The S

# THE STORY OF RUTH

Books on Biblical Subjects
by Isaac Asimov

WORDS IN GENESIS
WORDS FROM THE EXODUS
ASIMOV'S GUIDE TO THE BIBLE,
VOLUME ONE, THE OLD TESTAMENT
VOLUME TWO, THE NEW TESTAMENT
THE STORY OF RUTH

# the story of ruth

## BY

## ISAAC ASIMOV

222
As 4s

DOUBLEDAY & COMPANY, INC., GARDEN CITY, NEW YORK

22914

*To all the Ruths of the world*

# CONTENTS

You might expect the quotations in this book to be from the King James Bible, which is one of the traditional versions of the Bible. The King James Bible has been used by English-speaking Protestants for centuries and it is beautifully written. However, some of its words are old-fashioned, now, and a little hard to understand. In 1970, a new translation called The New English Bible was published, making use of more modern English. In this book, all my quotations will be from The New English Bible.

Those quotations from the Bible that are not from the book of Ruth are put in italics (*type that looks like this*), so that you can see at a glance what the Bible says and not confuse it with what I say. At the end of every such quotation I will make a little note, telling you the book, the chapter, and the verses. The quotation from Psalms—137:1–6—is from the book of Psalms, the 137th chapter, and verses 1–6, according to the traditional system of divisions used in the Bible. You can use the little note to look up the passage in the King James Bible, in The New English Bible, or in any translation; read it for yourself, and see what comes before and after if you are curious.

When a biblical quotation in this book includes three little dots like this (. . .), that means I am leaving out a few words that are unimportant. You can see what they are if you look up the quotation, and satisfy yourself that I am not changing the meaning of the quotation.

The passages I quote from Ruth are in the dark print called boldface (type that looks like this), so you can tell it at once from my own writing and from quotations from other places in the Bible. I will, little by little, quote the entire book of Ruth without leaving out a word. If you want to read the story just as the Bible has it, either before you read what I have to say, or after, just read the boldface parts in order, skipping everything in between. Sometimes it is useful to end a quotation from Ruth in the middle of a verse. For example, the quote from Ruth 1:18–19a means that I have stopped in the middle of verse 19. Since I include only the first part I call it 19a. In the next quotation I will include the rest of the verse which I will then label as 19b.

A word about the pronunciations in this book. I have put them in parentheses, and some of them are not descriptive of the Hebrew pronunciation. Elimelech, for example, has a pronunciation of e-LIM-ih-lek. The Hebrew pronunciation is more like EL-e-MEL-ekh. In this book, when I give pronunciations, they are the ones used commonly by English-speaking people.

ISAAC ASIMOV

# THE STORY OF RUTH

PART I

how Ruth came to
Be wRitten

CHAPTER 1

# EXILE TO BABYLON

In the Bible, there is a book called "Ruth" because it is about a girl with that name. It is quite short, but it interests us particularly these days, for it came to be written in order to deal with a problem that is now of world importance.

We don't know the name of the person who wrote the book, or where he got his material. We don't even know exactly when the book was written. The best estimate is that it was written somewhere between 450 B.C. and 380 B.C., or about twenty-five hundred years ago.

It was written in Judah, a small country to the west of the Dead Sea.

Long before the time in which Ruth was written, about 1000 B.C., in fact, a skillful warrior and political leader, named David, had become king of Judah. He went on to become king of Israel too, a larger nation of related people to the north of Judah.

David conquered the strong city of Jerusalem and

made it his capital. He also conquered the small surrounding nations of Moab, Edom, and Ammon. He extended his power northward as well.

By the time of his death in 973 B.C., he had built up an empire along the entire eastern Mediterranean coast. It included the territory on which the modern nations of Israel, Jordan, and Syria now stand.

David's son, Solomon, ruled over the empire in peace for forty years and built a great Temple in Jerusalem at which his subjects could worship. Shortly after Solomon's death in 933 B.C., however, the empire of David broke up. The northern portion broke away and formed the independent kingdom of Israel.

Judah shrank down into a small desert kingdom. Its capital was still at Jerusalem and the descendants of David still ruled there. It was poor and weak, however, and had great difficulty keeping its independence.

Still, it never forgot its great king, David, and the men of Judah always dreamed that someday his empire might be re-established.

That was just a dream though. Powerful nations had grown up in the East; nations far more powerful even than David's empire at its greatest. Before those nations, neither Judah nor Israel could stand.

The fiercest and most powerful of the eastern nations was Assyria. It had a large army and cruel monarchs who were eager for conquest and who punished rebellions fearfully. In 722 B.C. the nation of Israel was wiped out forever by the Assyrian king, Sargon II. The leading men of Israel were carried away into exile and never returned. The land became an Assyrian province.

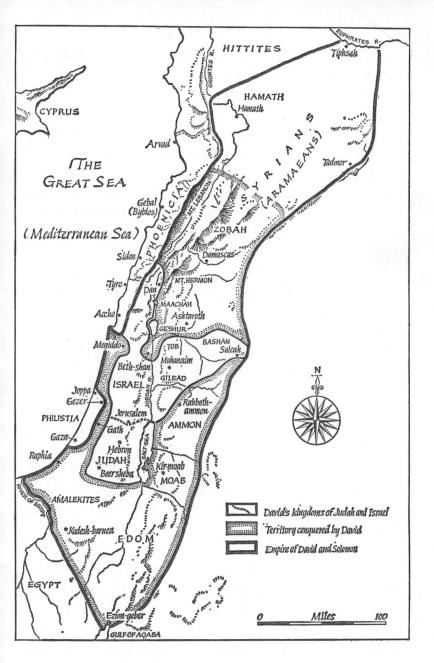

The empire of David and Solomon.

Judah, just to the south of Israel, was more fortunate and remained intact—but just barely.

In 701 B.C. an Assyrian army under its king, Sennacherib (sen-AK-uh-rib), laid siege to Jerusalem. It seemed certain that Jerusalem must fall since the Assyrians always beat down all obstacles in the path to victory.

Yet it did not fall. Jerusalem remained standing. Partly, this was because the Egyptians sent an army to help (for they feared the Assyrians might attack them next if Jerusalem fell). Partly, it was because a disease seems to have struck the Assyrian army and weakened it.

In any case, Sennacherib was content to accept a tribute. Then he marched away and Judah remained an independent kingdom.

In fact, it was still independent when Assyria finally fell before the onslaughts of other nations in 612 B.C. In the years that followed, with Assyria gone, Judah even expanded its territory.

But in place of Assyria, another conquering nation was established. The kingdom of Chaldea controlled all the territory along the Tigris and Euphrates rivers, territory that had once been Assyrian. The capital of the new empire was the ancient city of Babylon, and in its palace there ruled the king, Nebuchadrezzar (NEB-oo-kuh-DREZ-er).

Nebuchadrezzar and the Chaldeans did not intend to have independent nations on the Mediterranean shore. Such nations could be sources of trouble. Unless they paid tribute to Babylon, and bent low, and remained puppets of Nebuchadrezzar, they would be wiped out.

The kings of Judah weren't sure what they ought to do.

On the one hand they feared the mighty Nebuchadrezzar. On the other hand, to keep the great king of Chaldea happy, they had to pay out so much tribute that it kept the land impoverished.

Egypt, which feared the Chaldeans just as much as it had feared the Assyrians, encouraged Judah to rebel against Nebuchadrezzar. Finally, Judah did and the angry Chaldean king led a strong army against Jerusalem.

Perhaps the men of Judah (whom we usually refer to as Judeans, or, more commonly, as Jews) felt the city would be saved again as it had been in the time of Sennacherib. This time, though, it wasn't.

In 586 B.C. the Chaldean army finally broke through the walls and poured into Jerusalem. They smashed, burned, and looted. In particular, they destroyed the great Temple of Solomon.

In addition, they carried off thousands of the more important leaders of Judah to exile in Babylonia, as the land around the city of Babylon was called. They made Judah into a Chaldean province. It seemed that Judah was wiped out and would never rise again, just as Israel had been destroyed forever by the Assyrians a century and a half before.

Something unusual happened though. The Jews did not forget their land in their exile. They did not forget Jerusalem. Nor did they forget Mount Zion, on which the Temple had once stood.

In fact, one of them, whose name we don't know, wrote a moving song about the feelings of the Jews in exile. We can find it in the Bible now as the 137th Psalm. I will quote the first part of it here.

*By the rivers of Babylon we sat down and wept*
  *When we remembered Zion.*
*There on the willow-trees*
  *we hung up our harps,*
*for there those who carried us off*
  *demanded music and singing,*
*and our captors called on us to be merry:*
  *"Sing us one of the songs of Zion."*
*How could we sing the Lord's song*
  *in a foreign land?*
*If I forget you, O Jerusalem,*
  *let my right hand wither away;*
*let my tongue cling to the roof of my mouth*
  *if I do not remember you,*
*if I do not set Jerusalem*
  *above my highest joy.*

(Psalms 137:1–6)

The Jews in exile did not forget Jerusalem, the Temple, and their religion.

Fortunately for them, Nebuchadrezzar was an enlightened king in some ways and did not disturb them in their religious freedom. As long as they did not try to rebel or make disturbances they could worship as they pleased.

Of course, the Jews no longer had the Temple, but they had collected their traditions and their laws which, according to legend, had been given them by God through the great prophet Moses many centuries before.

They put together these traditions, in the form we now have them, in the first five books of the Bible. The Jews called these first five books the "Torah," which in English means the "Law."

The exiled Jews also collected some of the historical records of the times when Judah and Israel were independent lands. These became the biblical books of Joshua, Judges, 1 Samuel, 2 Samuel, 1 Kings, and 2 Kings. They collected the writings of certain great prophets which now make up such books as those of Isaiah, Jeremiah, Hosea, and Amos.

In later times they added still further books to the Bible, including the book we call Ruth. It wasn't till about 150 B.C. that the Bible came to exist in the complete form in which we have it today.

Groups of Jews would get together to read and study these books. Under the leadership of a prophet named Ezekiel, they worked out a system of worship that can be considered the beginnings of modern Judaism.

But always they waited for the chance of returning to Jerusalem. They never forgot Jerusalem.

# CHAPTER 2

# RETURN TO JERUSALEM

The chance to return finally came, for after Nebuchadrez-zar died in 562 B.C., the power of Chaldea declined. A new empire, that of Persia, arose in the north and east of Chaldea and it was under the rule of a great conqueror called Cyrus.

Unlike the Assyrian and Chaldean monarchs, Cyrus dealt leniently with the people he conquered, and the Jews in exile felt their hopes rise. If Cyrus conquered Babylon, perhaps he might be willing to allow the Jews to return to their own land.

In 539 B.C. Babylon fell. The Persian army marched in, but did not destroy the city. Cyrus kept his soldiers under control in accordance with his policy of tolerance.

It was not long before representatives of the Jewish exiles presented their petition, and Cyrus received them most kindly. He gave permission for those Jews who wished to do so to return to Judah and to rebuild the Temple in Jerusalem.

A number of Jews therefore began to make preparation for the journey to Jerusalem. Not all the Jews left Babylonia. Some were happy in the new land and had prosperous businesses there. They remained, but contributed goods and money to those who wished to return. In fact, a prosperous Jewish colony remained in Babylonia for over fifteen centuries after the time of Nebuchadrezzar.

The Jews who returned from exile did not, however, find matters easy. The land of Judah was by no means empty. There were people living there who were descended from Jews of the time before Nebuchadrezzar. After all, the Chaldean king had not taken everyone into exile, just a number of the leaders.

These people who had remained behind still worshiped the God of Israel, but did so in their own way. They did not use the particular rituals developed by the Jews in Babylon.

The people who had been in Judah all along had their chief center in the city of Samaria, which had once been the capital of the kingdom of Israel. After Jerusalem was destroyed by Nebuchadrezzar, Samaria became the important city of the land. The returning Jews therefore called the people living in the region "Samaritans."

When the returning Jews prepared to rebuild the Temple, the Samaritans offered to help. The Jews rejected that offer though. They felt that the Samaritan system of worship was wrong and that any temple built with their help would not be properly holy. For that reason, the Samaritans came to be the enemies of the Jews. The Samaritans built a temple of their own and a violent hatred arose between the two peoples, a hatred that lasted for centuries.

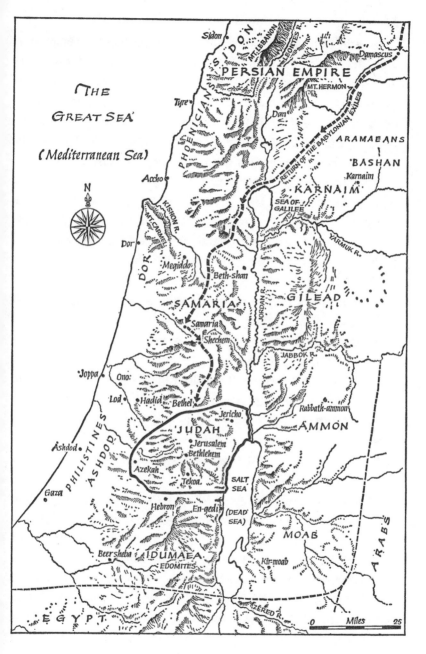

Jerusalem restored.

In addition, there were men of other faiths altogether who lived in the land. These had gods of their own and did not worship the God of Israel. In fact, many of them were descendants of those people whose lands had been conquered by David. They feared that if the Jews re-established themselves in Jerusalem, they might begin to think of once again building up David's empire.

The returning Jews found many enemies, therefore, who pleaded with the Persian authorities to keep the Temple from being rebuilt. The Jews had to keep negotiating with Cyrus and with later Persian kings in order to prevent local governors from stopping the rebuilding work. It was not until 516 B.C., twenty-two years after Cyrus had first given his permission, that a temple was finally dedicated in Jerusalem.

Even then, of course, it was a poor and unimpressive building. Those old men who were present and who could remember the glorious Temple of Solomon, which had been destroyed seventy years before, wept at the contrast.

The small party of Jews struggled on. They were protected by the Persian governors from the hostile people surrounding them, and they managed to continue services in their small Temple.

Yet it was difficult. According to the rules worked out in Babylonia, they had to observe certain rites. For instance, they had to keep the Sabbath one day every week. On this day they had to suspend all business and devote it entirely to worship.

This could be done if a Jew was part of a large community of Jews. All of them could suspend business together.

When Jews are few in number, however, and all the

non-Jews around are not observing the Sabbath but are conducting business on that day, then matters aren't so easy. Some Jews would then feel it necessary to do business on the Sabbath too, if only to compete.

In this respect, and in others as well, the new rules developed for Judaism in Babylonia began to weaken.

What about marriage and family life in the new Jerusalem, for instance?

Most of the Jews returning from exile were men. Where could they find wives?

It was natural for them to marry with the women of the land. These women, however, were not Jewish and knew little about the Jewish ways of worship. The husbands naturally did not stick so strictly to ritual if the wife was not Jewish. The children, too, were brought up more loosely, as far as religion was concerned.

More and more, then, the Jews of the new Jerusalem tended to be less and less Jewish.

# CHAPTER 3

# THE FOREIGN WIVES

Then, just as it began to appear that Judaism might not survive after all, even though the Temple had been rebuilt, there came a change.

Possibly about 450 B.C., after the new Temple had been standing for more than half a century, someone arrived from Babylonia. This was the priest Ezra, and it was he who forced the change.

Ezra was a specialist in the study of the Jewish Law. Such a specialist was called a "scribe." As the Bible says:

*He was a scribe learned in the law of Moses . . .*

(Ezra 7:6)

Ezra was horrified at the religious laxness of the men of Jerusalem and he at once organized a religious revival. He gathered together all the Jews of the region and read to them the Law. Here is how the Bible puts it:

*On the first day of the seventh month, Ezra the priest brought the law before the assembly, every man and woman, and all who were capable of understanding what they heard. He read from it, facing the square in front of the Water Gate, from early morning till noon, in the presence of the men and the women, and those who could understand; all the people listened attentively to the book of the law. Ezra the scribe stood on a wooden platform made for the purpose . . . Ezra opened the book in the sight of all the people, for he was standing above them; and when he opened it, they all stood . . .*

(Nehemiah 8:2–5)

What's more, Ezra had assistants in the form of priests, or "Levites," who explained some of the more difficult verses to groups in the audience.

*. . . the Levites expounded the law to the people while they remained in their places. They read from the book of the law of God clearly, made its sense plain and gave instruction in what was read.*

(Nehemiah 8:7–8)

This went on for a period of time, of course. The Bible, even just the first five books, could not be read and explained in a single day:

*And day by day, from the first day to the last, the book of the law of God was read. They kept the feast for seven days, and on the eighth day, there was a closing ceremony, according to the rule.*

(Nehemiah 8:18)

The revival was a great success and the fears that Judaism might just wither away were put to rest.

Concerning one thing Ezra was most insistent. He felt that what was most dangerous to Judaism was the tendency to intermarriage. As long as Jews married non-Jewish wives, there would always be the temptation to ease up on the ritual for the wife's sake. There would always be the chance that the children would not be brought up in truly Jewish fashion. After all, young children spend most of their time with their mother. If the mother was not Jewish, would the children be Jewish?

At least that was how it seemed to Ezra. As he tells the story in the Bible, he discovered the situation as soon as he came to Jerusalem. On his arrival, he said:

> . . . some of the leaders approached me and said, "The people of Israel, including priests and Levites, have not kept themselves apart from the foreign population . . . They have taken women of these nations as wives for themselves and their sons, so that the holy race has become mixed with the foreign population; and the leaders and magistrates have been the chief offenders."
>
> (Ezra 9:1-2)

Ezra was thunderstruck and horrified at this news. As a scribe of the law, he felt it taught that the Jews ought to avoid marrying with non-Jews if the religion was to be kept pure.

There were examples of this in the traditions concerning the earliest ancestors of the Jewish people, even concerning Abraham, the father of them all. The book of Genesis, the first book of the Bible, tells, for instance, of Abraham in his extreme old age, when he was worried about the future of his son Isaac. He called his servant to him and said to him:

> *I want you to swear by the Lord, the God of heaven and earth, that you will not take a wife for my son from the women of the Canaanites in whose land I dwell; you must go to my own country and to my own kindred to find a wife for my son Isaac.*
>
> (Genesis 24:3–4)

This was done, and Isaac married his cousin Rebecca. Eventually, Isaac and Rebecca had twin sons, Esau and Jacob. Esau married as he chose, without consulting his parents:

> *When Esau was forty years old he married Judith daughter of Beeri the Hittite, and Basemath daughter of Elon the Hittite; this was a bitter grief to Isaac and Rebecca.*
>
> (Genesis 26:34–35)

Rebecca was determined that Jacob must not follow this example.

> *Rebecca said to Isaac, "I am weary to death of Hittite women! If Jacob marries a Hittite woman like those who live here, my life will not be worth living." Isaac called Jacob, blessed him and gave him instructions. He said, "You must not marry one of these women of Canaan. Go at once to the house of Bethuel, your mother's father, in Paddan-aram, and there find a wife, one of the daughters of Laban, your mother's brother.*
>
> (Genesis 27:46, 28:1–2)

Jacob did as he was told, and it was from him that the Jews were descended, according to the biblical story. From Esau and his foreign wives there were descended the men of Edom, who were bitter enemies to the Jews.

Further cases occur later in the Bible, after enormous changes had overtaken the descendants of Jacob.

Jacob and his twelve sons eventually went to Egypt. At first, one of those sons, Joseph, was a great official among the Egyptians and all was well. In time, though, conditions changed and the descendants of Jacob, who grew very numerous, were enslaved. Because an alternate name for Jacob was Israel, these descendants were called "the children of Israel," or "Israelites."

After centuries of slavery, a leader named Moses appeared and managed to lead a large party of Israelites out of Egypt. He intended to take them back to Canaan where their ancestors, Abraham, Isaac, and Jacob, had lived. (It was the land of Canaan where the later kingdoms of Israel and Judah stood.)

There was difficulty here. The land was occupied by native Canaanites. In addition, new kingdoms had been established around the rim of Canaan. To the south was Edom (whose people were supposed to be descended from Esau) and to the east were Ammon and Moab (whose people were supposed to be descended from a nephew of Abraham).

All three kingdoms were suspicious of the army coming upon them from the desert. Moses assured the kingdoms that his army had no designs on their lands. He said that the Israelites merely wanted to march peacefully through their territory so that they could enter Canaan. The kingdoms did not trust such statements.

In the end, Moses found himself unable to enter Canaan directly from the south because of the opposition of Edom. He therefore led the Israelites the long way around and approached Canaan from the east.

There, Moab had been defeated in a war just a little while before and it was not in a position to resist the Israelites by force of arms. According to the tale as it appears in the Bible, the king of Moab did the next best thing. He hired a magician named Balaam (BAY-lam) to call down curses upon the Israelite army.

This tactic failed and the king of Moab then encouraged the women of the land to mix with the Israelite soldiers. In that way, they would lure them away from their own ways and weaken the Israelite army.

> When the Israelites were in Shittim, the people began to have intercourse with Moabite women, who invited them to the sacrifices offered to their gods; and they ate the sacrificial food and prostrated themselves before the gods of Moab.
>
> (Numbers 25:1–2)

Moses had to take strong measures against this, but the Israelites who had joined with the Moabite women refused to listen. The Israelite army came near to disaster in a kind of civil war and this was remembered later as very nearly the moment of greatest danger in the campaign to conquer Canaan.

As a result, of all the non-Jewish women represented as dangers to the faith of pious Jews, the Moabite women were somehow considered the worst. Indeed, when the Israelites finally attacked Moab at this time, Moses was angry at the fact that female prisoners had been spared and kept alive.

> *"Have you spared all the women?" he said. "Remember, it was they who, on Balaam's departure, set about seducing the Israelites into disloyalty to the Lord . . ."*
>
> (Numbers 31:15–16)

Many of the Moabite women were killed in consequence.

The hostility to Moab and to its sister-kingdom to the north, Ammon, is further shown in the book of Deuteronomy, the last of the five books of the Law. There the Bible has Moses say, in his summary of the Law:

> *No Ammonite or Moabite, even down to the tenth generation, shall become a member of the assembly of the Lord. They shall never become members of the assembly of the Lord, because they did not meet you with food and water on your way out of Egypt, and because they hired Balaam . . . to revile you. . . . You shall never seek their welfare or their good all your life long.*
>
> (Deuteronomy 23:3–6)

This passage makes it sound as though no Moabite or Ammonite is ever to be allowed to become a convert to Judaism.

All these stories of Abraham and Isaac, of Jacob and Esau, and of the women of Moab would surely have been in Ezra's mind as he considered the manner in which Jewish men were taking non-Jewish wives. He probably pointed out these stories in particular when he read the books of the Law to the assembled people. He may have pointed out the miseries that had followed intermarriage, how Esau had lost the chance to be the ancestor of the Jewish people, how Moses' army had lost so much strength because of the Moabite women.

Ezra called the people together, stood up, and announced to them:

> *"You have committed an offence in marrying foreign wives and have added to Israel's guilt. Make your confession now to the Lord the God of your fathers and do his will, and separate yourselves from the foreign population and from your foreign wives." Then all the assembled people shouted in reply, "Yes; we must do what you say . . ."*
>
> (Ezra 10:10–11)

And it was done. The foreign wives were put away and a large number of marriages were broken up.

# CHAPTER 4

# DAVID AND HIS PARENTS

One person at least must have disapproved so strongly of Ezra's policy that he decided to do something about it, to write a story to show that Ezra was wrong.

We don't know who he was. Let's just call him the Writer.

We don't know what went through the Writer's mind. Perhaps he considered the books of the Bible and noticed that although these did mention intermarriage with non-Jews with disapproval, there were also cases listed where such intermarriage led to no harm.

What about Joseph, the son of Jacob, who was prime minister of the king of Egypt, and the most powerful man in that great land? Whom did Joseph marry? Well, according to the Bible:

> *Pharaoh named him Zaphenath-paneah, and he gave him as wife Asenath the daughter of Potiphera priest of On.*

> (Genesis 41:45)

So Joseph married an Egyptian girl, who was even the daughter of a priest who worshiped idols. Yet this marriage was not mentioned with disapproval, nor did it come to evil. Joseph had two children by her.

> . . . *two sons were born to Joseph by Asenath the daughter of Potiphera priest of On. He named the elder Manasseh . . . He named the second Ephraim . . .*
>
> (Genesis 41:50–52)

Manasseh and Ephraim were considered by the Jews to be the ancestors of the tribes of those names. The tribes of Manasseh and Ephraim were the most powerful of those that made up the later kingdom of Israel, so that the men of that kingdom had to consider themselves descended from an Egyptian woman. In fact, Joshua, who conquered Canaan after the death of Moses, was of the tribe of Ephraim, so he was descended from an Egyptian woman, the daughter of a pagan priest.

The Writer may have felt, though, that people would argue that the kingdom of Israel had been destroyed by the Assyrians. Perhaps this showed that the descent from an Egyptian woman finally ruined them. What about the men of Judah then?

The Jews considered themselves descended, for the most part, from Judah, the fourth son of Jacob. The Bible clearly states that Judah had not hesitated to marry a non-Jewish woman. Speaking of Judah, the Bible says:

> . . . *he saw Bathshua the daughter of a Canaanite and married her.*
>
> (Genesis 38:2)

That might not do very well either, though, for of Judah's three sons by Bathshua, the two oldest died young. The third, Shelah, did have children and his descendants, stemming from a Canaanite woman, lived among the Jews as respected families in the time of the return from exile. The two most important clans of Judah, however, were considered to be descended from Perez and Zerah. These were the sons of Judah by another woman, Tamar. Tamar may have been a Canaanite woman too, but the Bible doesn't specifically say so.

The Writer may then have turned to the story of David himself; David, the great king.

David had been born as the seventh and youngest son of a family that lived in the city of Bethlehem, five miles south of Jerusalem. His father was a man of substance, owning herds of sheep and his name was Jesse.

That is about all that is known of David's ancestry as far as the older books of the Bible are concerned. Even the name of David's mother isn't given.

Just the same, there were probably traditions concerning David's ancestry, a line of descent that existed and was known even though it was not specifically written down in the older parts of the Bible. In The First Book of the Chronicles, which was probably written after the return from exile (it may even have been written by Ezra) this line of descent is given.

In the second chapter of The First Book of the Chronicles, Judah's sons are listed, including Perez, his fourth son and the one who was the ancestor of the most important Judean clan. Perez had two sons, of whom Hezron was the older. Then Hezron had three sons, of whom Ram was the second.

Ram was the father of Amminadab, who was the father of Nahshon, who was the father of Salma (or Salmon), who was the father of Boaz, who was the father of Obed, who was the father of Jesse.

The line of David's descent then was: Abraham, Isaac, Jacob, Judah, Perez, Hezron, Ram, Amminadab, Nahshon, Salma, Boaz, Obed, Jesse, David. The Writer probably knew this line of descent even if The First Book of the Chronicles had not yet been written in his time.

Next, the Writer may have noticed something that was rather odd in David's history.

In his youth, David had served in the army of King Saul, who ruled the northern tribes that made up Israel. The land of Judah was at that time dominated by the Philistines and patriotic Judeans would naturally flock to Saul, who was fighting those same Philistines.

David proved a most able officer. He won victories over the Philistines and became a favorite with the people. He also grew very friendly with Jonathan, the oldest son of Saul and heir to the throne. Saul, who was a suspicious man, began to wonder what David was up to. It was quite possible that David might be planning to help Jonathan seize the throne from his father. Or the young Judean might even be planning to use his popularity to seize the throne for himself.

Saul therefore planned to have David killed. Warned by Jonathan, however, David fled in time. He gathered a guerrilla band about himself and for some years remained an outlaw, hunted by Saul.

David knew that Saul was a ruthless man when moved by passion. If Saul failed to place his hands on David, he might take steps to have David's relatives killed. David's brothers might well be fighting with him in his band, but what about his old father and mother?

David therefore took steps to send them away to some secure place until the issue between himself and Saul was settled. The manner in which he did this is described in The First Book of Samuel:

> . . . *David went to Mizpeh in Moab and said to the king of Moab, "Let my father and mother come and take shelter with you until I know what God will do for me." So he left them at the court of the king of Moab, and they stayed there* . . .
>
> (1 Samuel 22:3–4)

David's caution apparently kept his parents safe. Eventually, Saul died in battle against the Philistines, and David, who was then allied to the Philistines, became king of Judah. Seven years later he became king of Israel too, and began building his empire.

The Bible doesn't tell us how long Jesse and his wife lived, so we don't know how much of their son's triumph they witnessed. Apparently, though, they died in peace, saved by their son's loyal concern for them.

But why should David have entrusted his parents to the king of Moab of all people? There was traditional enmity between the people of Moab on one side and those of Israel and Judah on the other. There was not only the matter of the events in the days of Moses and Balaam. There were later troubles too.

After Moses' death and the conquest of Canaan by his

successor, Joshua, there had been a period in which the
Israelites were not ruled by kings. They lived in more or
less independent tribes, each under its own leaders. Every
once in a while, a particularly capable leader made his
mark, leading one or more tribes against some enemy.
These leaders were called "judges" because one of their
functions was to judge disputes among the people of the
tribe they ruled.

During the time of the judges, there had been a time
when the Moabites under their king, Eglon, had invaded
Israelite territory:

> Once again the Israelites did what was wrong in the
> eyes of the Lord, and because of this he roused Eglon
> king of Moab against Israel. Eglon . . . advanced to
> attack Israel and took possession of the Vale of Palm
> Trees.
>
> (Judges 3:12–13)

The Vale of Palm Trees was in the territory of the tribe
of Benjamin. A man of that tribe, named Ehud, managed
to get admitted into the presence of the Moabite king,
and then assassinated him. With the Moabites disheart-
ened, the Israelites then attacked the occupying Moabite
army and destroyed it:

> . . . they seized the fords of the Jordan against the
> Moabites and allowed no man to cross. They killed
> that day some ten thousand Moabites, all of them men
> of substance and all fighting men; not one escaped.
> Thus Moab on that day became subject to Israel.
>
> (Judges 3:28–30)

With such a history of enmity between the two peoples, how could David be so confident that he could entrust his beloved father and mother to Moabites? How could he be sure that the Moabite king wouldn't have them killed, or perhaps sell them to Saul?

Was it that the king of Moab was at such enmity with Saul, that he would support any rebel against Saul? Or might it be that there was some family relationship between David and the Moabite king?

There was nothing in the Bible (as it existed in the time of the Writer) that spoke of any such relationship, but perhaps there were traditions about it. The Writer decided to make use of those traditions, whatever they were, and to fill them in with material from his own imagination where that was necessary.

In writing the story of David's ancestry he could then point out his objections to Ezra's policy of forbidding outside marriages.

# PART II

ruth

# CHAPTER 5

# NAOMI AND HER DAUGHTER-IN-LAW

It is this story of David's ancestry that is included in the biblical book Ruth and the Writer begins it in this fashion (as translated from the Hebrew, by those who prepared The New English Bible):

> **Long ago, in the time of the judges, there was a famine in the land, and a man from Bethlehem in Judah went to live in the Moabite country with his wife and his two sons.**
>
> **(Ruth 1:1)**

The Writer doesn't say in exactly what year this happened, but at no time in the Bible are years indicated. In ancient times, no one counted years the way we do today. At most, they described something as happening in the reign of a certain king, or after such and such a king had been reigning so many years. For this reason it is quite hard to date things closely in the Bible.

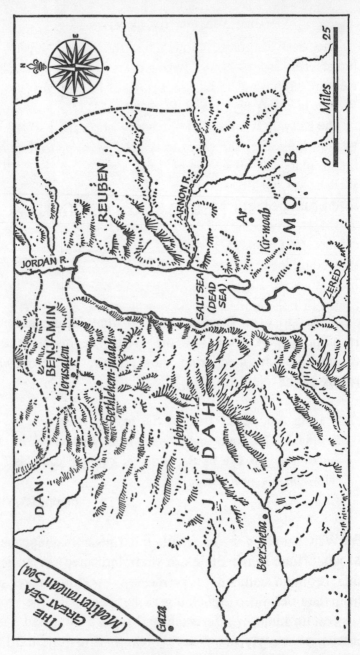

Judah and Moab in the time of Ruth.

The best estimate, though, is that the time of the judges ran from about 1200 B.C. to 1020 B.C. Perhaps we can suppose that by "in the time of the judges," the Writer is referring to a date of about 1150 B.C.

The very first words of the story show that Ruth was written long after the times in which it is supposed to have taken place. It took place "long ago." Actually, if the Writer was writing in Ezra's time, it took place about seven hundred years before.

But at any time the land of Israel and of Judah was subject to famine. There were few streams in the land that could be used as a water supply. Farmers depended on the rains. Every once in a while there would be less than normal rainfall. If there was considerably less, the crops would die and there would be a shortage of food. If it happened several years in a row, the reserve food would be used up and people would starve unless they could find someplace to go where there was food.

Numerous famines are recorded in the Bible. There was one in the time of David, for instance:

> *In David's reign there was a famine that lasted year after year for three years.*
>
> (2 Samuel 21:1)

But why should a famine drive this family from Judah to Moab? Moab was quite close to Judah, just on the other side of the Dead Sea. It was even more apt to suffer from lack of rain than Judah was. Surely if there was famine in Judah, there would be famine in Moab too.

Perhaps the Writer was just filling in detail at this point and was forced to use his imagination. It may be that the tradition he was working with simply told of a Judean family living in Moab—but why should such a family be living in the land of an enemy? The Writer felt he had to explain that so he used a famine as the reason.

He goes on to give some details:

> The man's name was Elimelech, his wife's name was Naomi, and the names of his two sons, Mahlon and Chilion. They were Ephrathites from Bethlehem in Judah. They arrived in the Moabite country and there they stayed.
>
> (Ruth 1:2)

The Judean family is described as being from Bethlehem. It was, after all, in Bethlehem that Jesse lived and where David was born. Thus, when Jesse is first mentioned in the Bible, it is when God is described as saying to Samuel, the last of the judges:

> ". . . I am sending you to Jesse of Bethlehem; for I have chosen myself a king among his sons."
>
> (1 Samuel 16:1)

Shortly after this passage, David is described as follows:

> David was the son of an Ephrathite called Jesse . . .
>
> (1 Samuel 17:12)

An Ephrathite is a man of Ephrathah, but, according to the Bible, Ephrathah is an older name for the town of Bethlehem. Thus, when one of Jacob's wives, Rachel, died, the event is described as follows:

*So Rachel died and was buried by the side of the
road to Ephrathah, that is Bethlehem.*

(Genesis 35:19)

The Writer is careful to describe the family about whom
he is telling the story as coming from Bethlehem and as
being Ephrathites so that the similarity with the biblical
description of David's origins is complete.

The names of the man and his wife are of the kind
that naturally would be used in those times. "Elimelech"
(e-LIM-ih-lek) is Hebrew for "God is king" and that is a
pious name to give a young Judean boy. "Naomi" means
"pleasure," the kind of name you would naturally give an
infant girl.

The names of the two sons are another thing altogether.
The meanings are not clear, but "Chilion" (KIL-ee-on)
seems to come from a Hebrew word for "weakness" while
"Mahlon" (MAY-lon) is from the word for "illness."
Surely, no one would give children such names.

It may be that this is another part of the story where
the Writer is using his imagination. The two sons are
doomed to die young and without children of their own
so the names are dramatically fitting. The tradition the
Writer was following did not give the real names of the
sons, apparently, so the Writer invented names.

The Writer does not say how Elimelech managed to get
along in Moab. Did he have relations there, or business
acquaintances? Did he own property there? To go into
that would have taken too much time and wasn't necessary.
The Writer had a point he was planning to make and he
wanted to concentrate on that.

Whatever the details, Elimelech and his family seemed

to get along well in Moab, for they stayed a considerable period of time and settled down. But important changes took place in the little family while they were in Moab:

> Elimelech Naomi's husband died, so that she was left with her two sons. These sons married Moabite women, one of whom was called Orpah and the other Ruth.
>
> (Ruth 1:3–4)

The meaning of "Orpah" (AWR-puh) is unknown. Perhaps the Writer didn't care much what he called her, since she plays very little part in the story. "Ruth" may come from the Hebrew word for "friend" and that is a good name, as we shall see.

The Writer does not say anything one way or the other about these Moabite marriages. He doesn't describe them as wicked or as good. He will let the reader judge for himself.

But further disaster strikes the family:

> They had lived there about ten years, when both Mahlon and Chilion died, so that the woman was bereaved of her two sons as well as of her husband.
>
> (Ruth 1:5)

This was indeed a frightening and terrible thing to happen to any woman, for in biblical days women had very few legal rights. They were property and belonged to some man. When a woman was young, she belonged to her father; when she was married, she belonged to her husband; when she was widowed, she belonged to her oldest son.

When a woman was old, widowed, and childless, and had no father, husband, or son, she was helpless. She couldn't inherit any of the property that might have belonged to the family. She couldn't do anything to make a living. She had to live on charity and be an object of pity or scorn.

Indeed, it was somehow considered to be a disgrace to be in such a position. The prophet, Isaiah, for instance, warned the people of Judah that if they behaved wickedly, their men would be slaughtered by their enemies. In order to point out in a dramatic way how many men would die, how many widows they would leave, how few survivors would be left, he said:

> *Then on that day seven women shall take hold of one man and say, "We will eat our own bread and wear our own clothes if only we may be called by your name; take away our disgrace."*
>
> (Isaiah 4:1)

The plight of the widow was so harsh and difficult, especially if she had no children or only very young ones, that the Bible is full of recommendations that she be shown special kindness. Thus, when the prophet Isaiah lists the deeds a good man should do, he says:

> *Cease to do evil and learn to do right, pursue justice and champion the oppressed; give the orphan his rights, plead the widow's cause.*
>
> (Isaiah 1:17)

Yet even though good men were urged to be kind to widows and help them in their troubles, it is always hard to share one's own possessions with the less fortunate. Probably few people heeded the prophet's advice.

Naomi, with no land, no property, no way of finding food, well knew how difficult it would be to go among her neighbors and beg. Even if they gave her something, surely it would be grudging, and she would feel humiliated.

For one thing her neighbors were Moabites (since she was living in Moab) and she was a Judean. Wouldn't they feel hostile to her and wonder why they should be expected to share their own small supplies of food with a stranger? Wouldn't they wonder why she didn't go back to her own people and be a burden to them? Mightn't they actually tell her to go back where she came from?

And indeed, there was a point to that. Strangers might feel no need to help, but surely the people of her own home town would feel differently. They would remember her as a child; they would remember her father and husband. They would surely be kind to her, especially now that the famine in Judah was long over.

With a sigh, then, the widowed Naomi decided to trudge the roads round the Dead Sea and return to Judah, a journey that was about fifty miles:

> Thereupon she set out with her two daughters-in-law to return home, because she had heard while still in the Moabite country that the Lord had cared for his people and given them food. So with her two daughters-in-law she left the place where she had been living, and took the road home to Judah.
>
> (Ruth 1:6–7)

The Writer doesn't bother to tell us in so many words that Naomi was a kind, good, and lovable woman. He doesn't have to. Her Moabite daughters-in-law loved her and that is a sure sign of Naomi's goodness since there are so many ways in which in-laws can quarrel, and so many occasions for them to hate each other. A mother can always be loved, whatever her failings; but for a mother-in-law to be loved, she must deserve it indeed.

Orpah and Ruth had sorrowed over their lost husbands and they grieved now to be losing their kind mother-in-law as well. They could not bear to let her go off alone, making her own way across the miles of country between Moab and her home. They could at least accompany her part of the way and help her when she wearied.

So that is what they did. On they went with her, past the farms, past the rocky hillsides, past the sheep that were cropping grass here and there.

Eventually, though, Naomi grew uneasy. How long were Orpah and Ruth going to accompany her? Perhaps the crucial moment came when they reached the Arnon River. This was the northern boundary of the small Moabite kingdom. North was the territory of Reuben, one of the smaller Israelite tribes.

That was enough, Naomi felt. Her daughters-in-law had done their duty and now they had to think of their own welfare.

**Then Naomi said to her two daughters-in-law, "Go back, both of you, to your mothers' homes. May the Lord keep faith with you, as you have kept faith with the dead and with me; and may he grant each**

of you security in the home of a new husband." She
kissed them and they wept aloud.

(Ruth 1:8–9)

Orpah and Ruth were, like Naomi, childless widows,
but they were still young. They were surely young enough
to marry again and have children. In fact, this was the
only goal they could now have. The position of women
was such that Orpah and Ruth simply had to find new
husbands.

But the young women were not thinking of such a
thing. They thought only that they loved their mother-
in-law and wanted to be with her. They told her what
their plans were. They had not just come to accompany
her part way after all:

Then they said to her, "We will return with you to
your own people."

(Ruth 1:10)

Naomi was at once alarmed. What could the girls be
thinking of? Did they think they could find husbands in
Judah? They were Moabite women after all. In Judah,
they would surely be outcasts, strangers. They would
be particularly despised because of the old story of how
the Moabite women tried to seduce the Israelite fighting
men in the days when Moses was trying to enter Canaan.

The Writer didn't have to explain this to the Jews of
his own time. They would know exactly what it meant
for someone to bring Moabite women into Judah.

It would be as though some American widow were
returning to the United States from Japan right after

World War II, with a young Japanese girl who was the widow of her son. If she were returning to some small home town, wouldn't she be certain that most of the people there would be hostile to a member of a nation they had so recently been fighting?

Naomi felt none of this prejudice against Moabite women herself. Her sons, after all, had married these girls and must have been happy with them. Now those girls were being faithful to her. —But what good was her own lack of prejudice? She had no way of making it useful to them, for she had no other sons to give them.

**But Naomi said, "Go back, my daughters. Why should you go with me? Am I likely to bear any more sons to be husbands for you? Go back, my daughters, go. I am too old to marry again. But even if I could say that I had hope of a child, if I were to marry this night and if I were to bear sons, would you then wait until they grew up? Would you then refrain from marrying? No, no, my daughters, my lot is more bitter than yours, because the Lord has been against me." At this they wept again.**

**(Ruth 1:11–13)**

Naomi stresses the fact that matters are worse for her than for the girls. Naomi is old and cannot have children, and can therefore never really expect to marry again and have the protection of a man. The girls, however, are still young and can yet find protection. Why, then, should they attach themselves to her? Why should they load themselves down with an unnecessary burden?

It made sense, really. Orpah, the widow of Chilion, the younger son, was persuaded.

> Then Orpah kissed her mother-in-law and returned
> to her people, but Ruth clung to her.
>
> (Ruth 1:14)

The two women must have watched Orpah on the road, walking reluctantly away, growing smaller with the distance, turning to wave one last time. And then Naomi spoke to Ruth, who still didn't seem to get it through her head that going to Judah would be the very worst thing she could do.

> "You see," said Naomi, "your sister-in-law has
> gone back to her people and her gods; go back with
> her."
>
> (Ruth 1:15)

That was a new point which Naomi was now making, and a very strong one, in her effort to persuade Ruth to act in her own best interests. In those early days, in the time of the judges, few Jews had yet come to take the view that there was one God who ruled the universe. Most of the people of Judah believed that every nation had its own god; each god powerful in its own land and over its own people. Each god protected its own people. For a person to go into a foreign land meant that he would leave the protection of his own god and have to rely on some strange god who might have no sympathy for him.

This is what Naomi is hinting to Ruth. If she won't

consider that in her own country she is much more likely to find a husband and security, let her remember that only in her own country can she be sure of the protection of her god.

Ruth, however, was stubborn and would listen to no arguments.

> "Do not urge me to go back and desert you," Ruth answered. "Where you go, I will go, and where you stay, I will stay. Your people shall be my people, and your God my God. Where you die, I will die, and there I will be buried. I swear a solemn oath before the Lord your God: nothing but death shall divide us."
>
> (Ruth 1:16–17)

Now Naomi could do nothing. Ruth was willing to abandon her people and her god. She would be a Jew and accept the God of Israel as her own.

Naomi, an older and more experienced woman, knew that this might not be enough. Prejudice will sometimes survive even so. Ruth might become a good Jew, yet still be looked down upon as Moabite by origin. There might even be those who would go along with the passage in the Law that said a Moabite could never become a Jew, no matter what.

And yet, what could Naomi do? Before the firm determination of the younger woman, she gave up.

> When Naomi saw that Ruth was determined to go with her, she said no more, and the two of them went on until they came to Bethlehem.
>
> (Ruth 1:18–19a)

Bethlehem was a small town, and it had no distinction in Israel at this time. Nothing much would ever happen there of importance to history until the birth of David, and that was still over a century in the future.

As might be expected in small towns, everybody knew everybody else. All except the young children had no trouble recalling Naomi and Elimelech and their two stalwart sons who, ten years before, had left a stricken Judah to try to make their way in the strange and hostile land of Moab.

Now Naomi was back, ten years older, with the lines of grief aging her face. But where was Elimelech? Where were her sons? And who was this strange young woman with her?

> **When they arrived in Bethlehem, the whole town was in great excitement about them, and the women said, "Can this be Naomi?"**
>
> **(Ruth 1:19b)**

Naomi could only feel bitter at their surprise, a surprise that was natural considering the way age and misfortune had changed her appearance and situation. And yet they were asking if this were indeed Naomi, which meant "pleasure." "Can this be Pleasure?" they were asking.

She could only reply sadly:

> **"Do not call me Naomi," she said, "call me Mara, for it is a bitter lot that the Almighty has sent me. I went away full, and the Lord has brought me back empty. Why do you call me Naomi? The Lord has**

pronounced against me; the Almighty has brought disaster on me."

(Ruth 1:20–21)

Naomi emphasizes her grief and bitterness here by asking to be called "Mara," a Hebrew word meaning "bitter."

And yet why did she say she had come back "empty?" Surely, she had not. She had with her a young and faithful woman who had followed her loyally from Moab. Could not this be counted in her favor?

Unfortunately not. Naomi had lost two sons, and sons were the pride of the family. It was they who inherited property, they who worked on the farm, they who won renown in war and council and in great deeds.

To have daughters was merely to have problems. A girl had to be taken care of and in the end the only good one could hope from her was to have her find some man who could take care of her.

In fact, Naomi might have said that she had come back from Moab worse than empty, for now she had a girl to be responsible for, and an alien girl too.

She did not say this. She loved Ruth too much to treat her as a liability. In fact, the best thing she could do would be to say nothing about her, to avoid drawing attention to her. That is what she did; she said nothing.

But for Ruth, standing there downcast, while all the women in town fluttered about Naomi, questioning, wanting the details, inquiring as to all that had happened, the arrival must have been hard. She could not help being aware of the curious sidelong glances in her direction, the hostility perhaps. It could scarcely have been a happy time for her.

> **This is how Naomi's daughter-in-law, Ruth the Moabitess, returned with her from the Moabite country.**
>
> **(Ruth 1:22a)**

# CHAPTER 6

# RUTH IN THE FIELDS

Yet not all was grim and hopeless. The famine, for instance, was gone. In this year, in particular, the rains had been copious and the fields of grain waved invitingly in the breeze. Both barley and wheat, the two grains of greatest importance, were doing well.

It was the month we call April now, a joyous month for farmers. The grain was almost ready to be harvested. The stalks bearing their heavy load were about to be cut down; the food supply for the year was assured.

Barley ripened and was ready for harvest first, and it was just at this pleasant season that Naomi and Ruth had reached Bethlehem.

> **The barley harvest was beginning when they arrived in Bethlehem.**
>
> **(Ruth 1:22b)**

Nor was Naomi entirely without resources. She had a family; at least her dead husband, Elimelech, had:

**Now Naomi had a kinsman on her husband's side, a well-to-do man of the family of Elimelech; his name was Boaz.**

(Ruth 2:1)

The name "Boaz" (BOH-az) is from a Hebrew word meaning "swiftness." Boaz must, indeed, have been the most important man in Bethlehem. He was the son and heir of Salma (or Salmon) and, following old traditions, Salma is listed in The First Book of the Chronicles as:

*. . . Salma the founder of Bethlehem . . .*

(1 Chronicles 2:51)

Presumably, Salma rebuilt the old town of Ephrathah, or enlarged it, and renamed it Bethlehem. He would then have been its leading citizen and its most prosperous farmer and Boaz would have succeeded him in these respects.

Yet pride would scarcely allow Naomi to go to the rich Boaz, begging, immediately upon arrival. It took an effort for a widow, who had been married to a hard-working farmer, whose two sons had also worked in the field, who had always eaten of her family's own food, to go asking for charity.

Perhaps, too, she felt Boaz might come to her. She felt he might remember his dead relative Elimelech, and feel some responsibility for the widow. By coming of his own accord, he might spare Naomi the pain and humiliation of asking.

Yet nothing happened. There might, of course, be an excuse for this. It was harvesttime, the very busiest time of the year for a farmer, and Boaz had broad acres. Perhaps after the harvest, he would remember.

But meanwhile, what could the two women do? Undoubtedly, the neighbors brought food, small contributions that made it possible for Naomi to set up some sort of comfort in some dwelling quarter which she may have rented, or which was granted her out of kindness. Still, the neighbors could not be expected to support her forever. They had their troubles too.

What, then, was to be done while Naomi waited for Boaz to remember his obligations?

That fact that it was harvesttime offered Naomi and Ruth one possible source of food.

The procedure of harvesting was as follows:

First, the reapers went across the field, each with his sickle, a sharp, curved knife. Seizing a handful of grain stalks, the reaper would bring down his sickle and cut them near the ground. He would leave the stalks lying in a bunch and pass on, seizing another handful of stalks, and thus going on. The sickle would rise and fall in swift, skillful motions and the field of grain would be mowed down.

Behind these reapers would come other men who would gather up the clusters of cut stalks and bind them with one of these stalks into a "sheaf" that was easy to handle. Then still others would come who would pick up the sheaves and pile them together into large "shocks."

In this procedure, there was always some imperfection. Some stalks might be missed by the sickle. Or some stalks which were cut down might be missed by the binder.

Of course, if the reapers and binders worked very slowly and carefully, they would not miss a single stalk, but why bother to do that? By working very rapidly they might leave behind a small proportion of the stalks, but it was important to complete the harvest as quickly as possible. To lose the time necessary to gather up a few missed stalks was foolish.

Besides, it was customary to allow poor people to go through the fields after the reapers and binders had gone their way, so that they could pick up any stray stalks they might find and keep them. This was called "gleaning." Such gleaning might be all that stood between the poor and hunger, and it would be cruel for a prosperous farmer, who was assured of his own food, to work his men overtime in order to keep poor people from the handfuls of grain they might gather.

In fact, it was a humane feature of the Law that the harvesters were ordered to make no effort to gather up every last grain. They were not even to make any effort to reap the grain at the edges of the field. The Bible says:

> *When you reap the harvest of your land, you shall not reap right into the edges of your field; neither shall you glean the loose ears of your crop . . . You shall leave them for the poor and the alien.*
>
> (Leviticus 19:9–10)

This same rule is repeated later in the book of Leviticus and again in the book of Deuteronomy. It is emphasized by being said three times.

With harvest about to begin, then, there was the possibility of gaining a little food by gleaning.

> **Ruth the Moabitess said to Naomi, "May I go out to the cornfields and glean behind anyone who will grant me that favour?"**
>
> **(Ruth 2:2a)**

Ruth was realistic, you see. Even though the Law said that fields might be gleaned by the poor and even by the alien, not everybody adhered to the Law. Some farmers were sure to be greedy enough to insist that all their stalks be scrabbled together. They might feel resentful of the poor people who would come swarming over their land to gather part of what the farmer felt was really his. He might order his harvest hands to drive such people away.

Ruth knew it would be wiser to ask permission humbly before attempting to glean.

Perhaps Naomi was aware of other dangers that Ruth didn't properly appreciate. Ruth was a young and unprotected woman, undoubtedly pretty, and she would go out in the fields among a group of harvest hands. Even if she were a woman of the region, that might not protect her from coarse jokes or from mistreatment of one kind or another. But she was a Moabite woman.

Would anyone care what happened to a Moabite woman? Would anyone try to protect her? Was it at all safe to let her go to the fields alone? Naomi had to ask herself that.

Then, too, gleaning was hard, backbreaking work. The stalks were scattered about; they had to be picked up one by one and placed in a basket. All day long, in the hot sun, a gleaner would have to be peering about in this place and that, with other gleaners competing with her, rushing for stalks to get them before she did.

In the end, a poor woman would work much harder for her handful of grain than any of the strong young men in the field would in their ordinary harvesting.

Naomi was too old to glean in the fields or she would have gone herself. She surely would not have asked Ruth to undertake such hard and dangerous work.

It was Ruth, however, who offered of her own free will to go. She stood there, young and straight, before her mother-in-law and asked for permission to undertake the task so that they might eat.

Naomi had experience with Ruth. She knew that no amount of argument would persuade Ruth to take the easy way out. Ruth was politely asking permission as was proper for a daughter-in-law, but Naomi knew there was no way of denying that permission.

With Ruth, loyalty came first. She had insisted on coming to Bethlehem with Naomi, and she would insist on doing whatever had to be done to care for the older woman. What, then, could Naomi do but give permission?

**"Yes, go, my daughter," she replied.**

(Ruth 2:2b)

Ruth did not hesitate. In fact, she couldn't. Harvest-time would not last forever.

> So Ruth went gleaning in the fields behind the reapers. As it happened, she was in that strip of the fields which belonged to Boaz of Elimelech's family . . .
>
> (Ruth 2:3)

Was it purely coincidence?

Perhaps it was, for Naomi had apparently said nothing about Boaz to Ruth. Perhaps Naomi had not wanted to raise false hopes in her daughter-in-law's heart, for their lot might seem all the harder when those hopes were disappointed. Or perhaps she could not bring herself to admit to Ruth that she had a rich relative who might be so hard-hearted and unfeeling as to leave them in poverty. The Moabite girl might wonder if that was what all Judean people were like.

So Ruth went out gleaning without any hint as to the fact that some particular piece of land might belong to a relative.

On the other hand, there could be a good reason why she should end up in Boaz's farmland.

We can picture her as going out to the fields, hurrying past the harvesters getting ready to do their work. It is the break of day; they are having their morning meal, perhaps, or else sharpening their sickles and preparing their other equipment.

They would see the young girl, hastening along with her basket, and they would know her, of course. She was just a Moabite girl, and alien. They might perhaps call out to her, make rough remarks, or hateful sneers about her nationality. They might order her to stay away from their fields.

The Law said that the poor and the alien should not be barred from the fields, but perhaps not everyone was as tolerant as the Law ordered them to be. The Law, in fact, forbade harshness of any kind toward aliens, saying:

> *You shall not oppress the alien, for you know how it feels to be an alien; you were aliens yourselves in Egypt.*
>
> (Exodus 23:9)

Just the same, it is hard to overcome prejudice and Ruth must have felt the pangs of it as she tried to find a place where she might be permitted to glean.

As it will soon turn out though, Boaz was a kind and pious man, one who would surely obey the merciful dictates of the Law and who would, furthermore, insist that those who worked for him do so too.

When Ruth came to the part of the farms in which the men of Boaz were getting ready to work, there would have been no rude remarks; there might have been friendly smiles instead. Naturally, then, she would stop and ask courteously, with her Moabite accent, if it would be all right if she gleaned.

Permission would have been given and there it was she began to work. It wouldn't be such a coincidence after all.

Later in the day, when the work was well advanced, Boaz arrived in the field:

> . . . and there was Boaz coming out from Bethlehem. He greeted the reapers, saying, "The Lord be with you"; and they replied, "The Lord bless you."
>
> (Ruth 2:4)

These were simple times and the landowners were not yet so high and mighty that they did not work in the fields along with their hired men—or at least come to supervise.

It was important to do so, for men are not as likely to work as industriously and efficiently for others as they would for themselves. Furthermore, when many men are working, someone is needed to make decisions, to relieve this man and push on that one, to hurry the work in one place or to change its nature in another.

For this purpose, a landowner might, of course, hire an overseer, some special servant of greater intelligence and force than others; one who could make decisions and hasten the work. It would be the responsibility of the overseer to see that the work was done well and quickly.

And yet even then it would have helped if the overseer knew that he would be under the keen eye of the landowner himself now and then. In fact, if the owner was kindly and enlightened, as Boaz was, he would have been aware of the fact that an overseer, eager to get the work done thoroughly and well (and earn a bonus for himself, perhaps) was likely to drive the hired men under him too harshly.

It would pay an owner who sees further than his own immediate interests to prevent this; to see to it that the overseer encourages efficiency and industry, but not with such harshness as to produce rebellion. A happy workforce produces more in the long run than one driven by the lash.

So when Boaz greets the reapers, they are glad to see him and reply, "The Lord bless you."

Boaz stands there in the sun, his bronzed farmer's face looking out over the fields, taking in the general situation and, no doubt, finding it satisfactory. He notes, too, several poor people gleaning in the fields after the reapers and suddenly his eyes narrow. There is one there whom he doesn't recognize and for him not to recognize anyone in Bethlehem was most unusual. In astonishment, he turned to his overseer, who has probably been making his report on the morning's work—

> Then he asked his servant in charge of the reapers, "Whose girl is this?"
>
> (Ruth 2:5)

The overseer looked up to see whom it was that Boaz was asking about.

> "She is a Moabite girl," the servant answered, "who has just come back with Naomi from the Moabite country. She asked if she might glean and gather among the swathes behind the reapers. She came and has been on her feet with hardly a moment's rest from daybreak till now."
>
> (Ruth 2:6–7)

The overseer was not unkind in his explanation, but he had to point out that Ruth was a Moabite. It was the first thing about her that would strike anyone in Bethlehem. She was a foreigner, an alien.

Yet it had to be admitted she was a hard worker. She had been searching and bending and gathering the stalks one by one for hours.

Boaz could not help being moved. He knew very well that Naomi was the widow of Elimelech, his relative. The story of her arrival had spread throughout the town and had reached him. He knew that she had brought a young daughter-in-law who had refused to abandon her but who had linked her own young fate with that of the older woman.

And now here was the daughter-in-law, working endlessly in the hot sun for just a little grain with which to support herself and her mother-in-law, and he himself had done nothing. To be sure, there had not been much time as yet, and he had been very busy, but the fact was he had done nothing. Embarrassed and ashamed, he came up to Ruth to speak to her.

Ruth must at once have ceased working when the owner of the land approached her. Was he going to order her away? Anxiously, she waited for him to speak.

> Then Boaz said to Ruth, "Listen to me, my daughter: do not go and glean in any other field, and do not look any further, but keep close to my girls. Watch where the men reap, and follow the gleaners; I have given them orders not to molest you. If you are thirsty, go and drink from the jars the men have filled."
>
> (Ruth 2:8–9)

Ruth was thunderstruck. She had not been in Bethlehem long, but she must already have experienced the hostility toward any Moabite woman. She must have seen the suspicious looks from the women, the hard amusement from the men, the whispers just out of earshot. She must even have felt the sting of the thoughtless taunts from the children.

Perhaps she even wondered sadly if the reason Naomi was not receiving more help from the neighbors, the reason no relatives came to visit, was because of the disapproval of the older woman's having brought a Moabite girl into Bethlehem.

All this she endured because Naomi spoke to her always with love, addressed her always as her daughter.

And now here was this important man, this wealthy landowner with his kind look, speaking similarly to her and calling her "my daughter." Was it possible he didn't know that she was a foreigner?

Ruth did not want to impose on him with false pretences:

> She fell prostrate before him and said, "Why are you so kind as to take notice of me when I am only a foreigner?"
>
> (Ruth 2:10)

It was a fair question. Boaz reached down to help her up and answered as fairly and openly:

> Boaz answered, "They have told me all that you have done for your mother-in-law since your hus-

**band's death, how you left your father and mother
and the land of your birth, and came to a people you
did not know before. The Lord reward your deed:
may the Lord the God of Israel, under whose wings
you have come to take refuge, give you all that you
deserve."**

**(Ruth 2:11–12)**

It was a great relief to Ruth to hear these words. He
certainly knew she was a foreigner, a Moabite, but he
seemed to approve of her the more for it. He felt it a
noble deed that she had sacrificed her own family,
people, and god, and accepted those of her mother-in-
law out of love.

Yet one thing disturbed her. This man who had
approached her so kindly was not a young man, but
neither was he very old. And he was a rich man who
could afford more than one wife (for in the early days
of Israelite history, it was quite usual for important men
to have many wives).

Indeed, not only could a wealthy man have more than
one wife, he could also treat women servants as though
they were wives, except that they did not have the usual
honor and respect that legal wives had. They were merely
"concubines" and "handmaidens."

The position of these handmaidens was not a high
one, and foreign girls, in particular, might be taken as
a handmaiden instead of a wife.

If Boaz wanted to take Ruth as a handmaiden, she
could scarcely resist, for women with no males to protect them had no rights in this respect. Everyone would

consider Ruth lucky that Boaz took any kind of notice of her.

And yet Ruth did not want to be a mere handmaiden when, in the past, she had been the beloved wife of a man of Judah. Besides it would mean that she would be parted from Naomi, and who would then look after the older woman? (She did not, of course, know that Boaz was a relative of Naomi.)

Ruth could only appeal, respectfully, to Boaz's kindness.

> **"Indeed, sir," she said, "you have eased my mind**
> **and spoken kindly to me; may I ask you as a favour**
> **not to treat me only as one of your slave-girls?"**
>
> **(Ruth 2:13)**

The Writer does not tell us what Boaz answered, but he must have assured her he had no evil intent upon her, for Ruth showed no fear of him during the remainder of the day.

In fact, Boaz went out of his way to treat Ruth with respect and kindness. The time had come to pause in the day's occupation for the midday meal, after which work could be resumed with renewed strength.

Ordinarily, the reapers felt no responsibility for the gleaners. The gleaners were there out of charity and might have brought a few mouthfuls of food with them, or might return home for what they could find there. The reapers didn't care.

Boaz was careful, however, to see that Ruth, who had been working so hard all morning, was not left to her own devices.

When meal-time came round, Boaz said to her, "Come here and have something to eat, and dip your bread into the sour wine." So she sat beside the reapers, and he passed her some roasted grain. She ate all she wanted and still had some left over.

(Ruth 2:14)

The reapers must have been curious indeed at the kind treatment thus offered Ruth by the rich farmer who hired them. Or perhaps they remembered that Boaz was a relative of Naomi's dead husband.

The meal was over finally. Ruth took what still remained of what she had been given and placed it in a pouch to take back with her. She then returned to her gleaning.

Boaz's kindness toward the girl continued, however. He looked after her, then turned to his men:

When she got up to glean, Boaz gave the men orders. "She," he said, "may glean even among the sheaves; do not scold her. Or you may even pull out some corn from the bundles and leave it for her to glean, without reproving her."

(Ruth 2:15–16)

Ordinarily, gleaners could only work over a field after the sheaves had been carried off. If the sheaves were still there, it would be too easy for a gleaner to pull stalks out of them and take grain that belonged to the farmer. Certainly, any gleaner caught doing that would be forced to give it back or would, perhaps, be chased off the field altogether.

But this was exactly what Boaz forbade his men to do. If Ruth wanted to take from the sheaves themselves, she was to be allowed to do so. In fact, what if Ruth did not take from the sheaves, even if she had the chance, out of fear, or out of respect for the farmer's property? In that case, the men were deliberately to allow grain to fall in her path, making it look like an accident.

It was really a most delicate act on the part of Boaz. Had he simply laden her down with grain to carry home, it might have looked as though he were trying to win her regard in order that she might willingly become his handmaiden.

What he was doing instead was seeing to it that she would have considerable grain and yet making it appear that it was entirely through her own labors that she had it and not through his charity at all. In that way, she would not feel beholden to him. He remembered her uneasiness when she asked him not to treat her as a slave-girl and he was intent on showing her that he would not.

Boaz's kindly intention worked perfectly. Ruth may have wondered at the carelessness of the reapers, but may have decided that that was the way it was in the land of Judah. The reapers there, she may have decided, were not as careful as the men of Moab. In any case, she ended with an extraordinary amount of stalks.

These she beat in order to knock off the ears of grain, for it was only the ears that were useful. There would be no point in trying to carry the useless stalks as well all the way back to Naomi's poor home. Ruth ended with an enormous quantity of ears of barley.

So Ruth gleaned in the field till evening, and when she beat out what she had gleaned, it came to about a bushel of barley. She took it up and went into the town, and her mother-in-law saw how much she had gleaned.

(Ruth 2:17–18a)

Naomi's first feeling when she saw Ruth that evening must have been one of thankfulness that she was safely home. We can be pretty sure she had spent a restless day wondering if Ruth might not perhaps be mistreated.

It was only after that that she must have looked at the basket Ruth put down and seen it overflowing with rich ears of barley.

Ruth may not have known what the reaping habits of the Bethlehem harvest hands were, but Naomi certainly did. Naomi knew with absolute certainty that it was impossible for anyone to go out into the fields and come back with anything like a bushel of barley.

And then Ruth, still without knowing anything was unusual, began to bring out the roasted grain that she had carefully saved from her midday meal.

Then Ruth brought out what she had saved from her meal and gave it to her.

(Ruth 2:18b)

That was the last straw. Not only had she collected an enormous amount of grain, but she had obviously been invited to share in the reapers' meal. What had happened? How had it come about? What was the reason for the obvious kindness with which Ruth had been treated?

> Her mother-in-law asked her, "Where did you glean
> today? Which way did you go? Blessings on the
> man who kindly took notice of you." So she told her
> mother-in-law whom she had been working with,
> "The man with whom I worked today," she said, "is
> called Boaz."
>
> (Ruth 2:19)

Naomi was thunderstruck. To herself she had to acknowledge that her harsh feelings against this relative of hers had been without foundation. He had known about her and about Ruth and he was taking a way of helping her that would carry no air of charity about it at all.

> "Blessings on him from the Lord," said Naomi,
> "the Lord has kept faith with the living and the
> dead. For this man is related to us and is our next-
> of-kin."
>
> (Ruth 2:20)

Now at last Ruth learned of the relationship. So that was why Boaz had been so kind. It was not merely because he was enticed by her pretty face and wanted her as his handmaiden.

To be sure, he had behaved very properly all that day and had given her no cause for alarm, and yet she must have thought that if she returned to the same field day after day, she would be tempting him. He might forget his good intentions and suspect her of trying to rouse his interest in her. For that reason, she might have been considering a trip to some other field the next day.

But now the situation was different. She told Naomi of a further act of kindness on the part of Boaz.

> "And what is more," said Ruth the Moabitess, "he told me to stay close to his men until they had finished all his harvest."
>
> (Ruth 2:21)

Naomi agreed with this at once. In fact, to Naomi it seemed that Ruth must on no account insult Boaz by making it appear that she was suspicious of his good intentions. That would ruin a plan that was now building in Naomi's mind.

> "It is best for you, my daughter," Naomi answered, "to go out with his girls; let no one catch you in another field."
>
> (Ruth 2:22)

Ruth did precisely as she was told. Nor did Boaz take her into his own house as a handmaiden or a slave-girl. He left her strictly free and so she could stay with Naomi, sharing with her constantly of what she gained through gleaning:

> So she kept close to his girls, gleaning with them till the end of both barley and wheat harvest; but she lived with her mother-in-law.
>
> (Ruth 2:23)

The wheat grew ripe about two weeks after the barley and the whole time of harvesting lasted about seven weeks. By that time, Ruth was well tanned through her work in the fields and was probably known to all the people of Bethlehem as an industrious, cheerful, and sweet girl, modest, virtuous, and unassuming.

The fact that Boaz saw to it that she was well treated, yet did not take advantage of her, must have led many others to treat her with decent respect as well. The fact that she was a Moabite girl seemed not so important after all.

CHAPTER 7

# NAOMI'S PLAN

As for Naomi, she was more and more pleased with
Ruth, with her behavior and with the success she was
having in adjusting to life in Bethlehem. Naomi was
hoping for a successful completion of the harvest, when
all the land would be joyous in the midst of plenty, and
there would be a time for feasting.

Indeed, two of the three great feasts of Israelite
traditions were closely connected with this spring harvesting.

The great feast of the Passover, which, according to
later tales, celebrated the anniversary of the liberation
from Egypt, fell at the beginning of the spring harvest.
Next came the great feast of the completed harvest which
was celebrated seven weeks later. It was called the "Feast
of Weeks" because its time was set by counting the
weeks after Passover. In Hebrew the festival was called
"Shabuoth" for that means "weeks" in English.

The Law said:

*Seven weeks shall be counted: start counting the seven weeks from the time when the sickle is put to the standing corn; then you shall keep the pilgrim-feast of Weeks to the Lord your God and offer a free-will offering in proportion to the blessing that the Lord your God has given you. You shall rejoice before the Lord your God, with your sons and daughters, your male and female slaves, the Levites who live in your settlements, and the aliens, orphans and widows among you.*

(Deuteronomy 16:9–11)

It was a time of general rejoicing, then, that was coming; a time when even widows and aliens might rejoice and be welcomed into the fold in the common delight at the good harvest. At such a time, all would be in a kindly mood and a daring venture might work which would not succeed at another time.

So Naomi, who must have been spending weeks thinking about the matter, decided the time had come. It had to be done now if it were to be done at all.

Ruth had been good to her, as good as any natural daughter could be, and she felt it necessary to be responsible for the welfare of the young woman in turn.

**One day Ruth's mother-in-law Naomi said to her, "My daughter, I want to see you happily settled. Now there is our kinsman Boaz: you were with his girls. Tonight he is winnowing barley at his threshing-floor."**

**(Ruth 3:1–2)**

Once the stalks of grain were all collected, the ears had to be removed and collected. Small quantities could be beaten as Ruth had beaten what she had gleaned. The process was called "threshing" and it could be done on a "threshing-floor," a dry, hard, flat piece of ground.

A small quantity might be beaten out with a "flail," a long stick to which a shorter, flattened stick was attached by a hinge. To take care of larger quantities a wooden sledge was used. To its bottom were fixed knobs of stone or metal and this would be drawn round and round the threshing-floor by oxen.

It was a sign of the humaneness of the Law that it had regard even for the oxen who did the threshing. The Law said:

> *You shall not muzzle an ox while it is treading out the corn.*
>
> (Deuteronomy 24:4)

After all, the grain was food for oxen and it would be cruel to have the animal work so hard, conscious of the grain at all times and be unable to eat. By leaving the ox unmuzzled he could "glean," so to speak, as the poor could.

The beating or scraping loosened the ears of grain and broke up the stalks and straw. When threshing was done, there was a mixed heap of ears and of chopped stalks and straw ("chaff") on the ground.

The mixture was separated, or "winnowed," by being lifted on a many-tined "winnowing fork" and tossed into the air. The wind would catch the light chaff and blow it away. The heavy grains of barley or wheat would fall back on the ground and when all the chaff was gone the ears would be collected.

The work was lighter than reaping had been; the harvest was almost over; the Feast of Weeks was at hand. It was a time of joy.

Ruth knew this; for it was much the same in Moab. But what was it that was in Naomi's mind? Ruth did not have long to wait, for Naomi went on:

> "Wash and anoint yourself, put on your cloak and go down to the threshing-floor, but do not make yourself known to the man until he has finished eating and drinking. But when he lies down, take note of the place where he lies. Then go in, turn back the covering at his feet and lie down. He will tell you what to do."
>
> (Ruth 3:3–4)

Ruth understood at once; so did the audience who read the tale and who listened to it when it was first written. What was involved was an old, old custom that was designed to protect widows; a custom that dated back to the earliest days of Israelite history.

The early Israelites had a strong sense of family, as is true of most tribal societies. It was the family, rather than the individual, that counted. Possessions belonged to the family as a whole, and no person was truly dead if he left sons behind who could inherit the possessions and hold the ancestral name in reverence. This was one of the reasons why it was so distressing for a man to die without sons. It was a much more real death that way.

The Law guarded against this and said:

*When brothers live together and one of them dies without leaving a son, his widow shall not marry outside the family. Her husband's brother shall . . . take her in marriage and do his duty by her as her husband's brother. The first son she bears shall perpetuate the dead brother's name so that it may not be blotted out from Israel.*

(Deuteronomy 25:5–7)

In this way, the widow kept her position as a legal wife; she was no concubine or handmaiden. What's more, her son could then inherit her first husband's property. It was a kind of legal continuation of the first marriage, giving the widow security and the dead husband remembrance.

This custom was called "levirate marriage" from the Latin word *levir* meaning "husband's brother."

The best-known and earliest example of this custom involved Judah himself. He was the fourth son of Jacob and the man who was considered to be the ancestor of the people of Bethlehem and all the other towns of the tribe of Judah.

Judah had three sons: Er, Onan, and Shelah, and the Bible says:

*Judah found a wife for his eldest son Er; her name was Tamar. But Judah's eldest son Er was wicked in the Lord's sight, and the Lord took his life. Then Judah told Onan to sleep with his brother's wife, to do his duty as the husband's brother and raise up issue for his brother.*

(Genesis 38:6–8)

Onan, however, refused to do his dead brother this service and he died too. Judah was reluctant, then, to marry Tamar to his third son, Shelah, feeling that the woman was "bad luck" and that his third son might die too.

Tamar, remaining a widow and resenting this lowly estate, used trickery to force Judah himself to give her children. At first, Judah was in a rage, but then he said:

> "She is more in the right than I am, because I did not give her to my son Shelah."
>
> (Genesis 38:26)

This old legend about Judah points out how this respected ancestor valued the institution of the levirate marriage. It also shows how Onan was punished by God for refusing his part in it.

The Bible also points out how well this particular incident turned out, for Tamar had twin sons, of which Judah was the father. These were named Perez and Zerah, and they were the ancestors of the most important clans among the descendants of Judah.

What's more, it was from Perez that Boaz was descended. Boaz himself, then, was descended of a levirate marriage.

To be sure, there were disadvantages to the levirate marriage. Often, the husband's brother, who had to do his duty to his dead brother's widow, was himself already married and might have children of his own. Then there might be competition and quarreling between the wives and between the two sets of children.

Even if the dead husband's brother was not married, he may have felt that any children that resulted would not be counted as his own and he would still be left childless as far as inheritance was concerned. This was Onan's concern, for as the Bible says:

*Onan knew that the issue would not be his.*
(Genesis 38:9)

Levirate marriage could only work in a polygamous society, one in which it was possible for a man to take more than one wife. Of course, Israel was polygamous in earlier centuries. David himself had many wives. His son, Solomon, was supposed to have no less than a thousand wives and concubines.

Polygamy had its problems, however, and there were always movements to have a society in which every man was allowed only one wife—a condition called "monogamy."

The Law was not finally put into writing until the time of the Exile, and while it contained some customs that may have been a thousand years old or more by that time (such as levirate marriage) it also had newer ways of thinking in it too.

For instance, the notion grew that it was wrong for a woman to be married to two brothers (or for marriages between close relatives to take place at all). In one place the Law says:

*If a man takes his brother's wife, it is impurity.*
(Leviticus 20:21)

This seems to go against the institution of the levirate marriage. It might mean a man couldn't marry his brother's wife while he was still alive, or if she already had sons, but it doesn't say so exactly. This could lead to confusion.

Then, too, there were movements to make the laws of inheritance more liberal, so that it wouldn't be so necessary to have levirate marriages. Suppose a man died and left only daughters. If they could not inherit, being women, then a levirate marriage was necessary. But what if they could inherit. So the Law included a later development in this direction and says:

> "When a man dies leaving no son, his patrimony shall pass to his daughter. If he has no daughter, you shall give it to his brothers. If he has no brothers, you shall give it to his father's brothers. If his father has no brothers, then you shall give possession to the nearest survivor in his family, and he shall inherit."
>
> (Numbers 27:8–11)

But what if a man died without children at all, neither sons nor daughters? This liberalized law of inheritance still did not allow for widows, and this could set up family squabbles. A childless widow might want the security afforded by marriage and she would insist on her brother-in-law taking care of her and giving her children. She would cite one part of the Law for that. The brother-in-law might, on the other hand, refuse to do so, saying his dead brother's property was now his and there was no reason he should risk it by giving the widow children who would then inherit that property instead of him. He would take Onan's view, you see.

By the Writer's time, polygamy had died out in Judah and so had the whole institution of levirate marriage, so Jews in his time didn't worry about these particular contradictions in the Law.

Not so in the time of Naomi and Ruth. The levirate marriage still existed, but it had to be handled delicately. There were many reasons why a next-of-kin might refuse to honor it. In fact, as we shall see later, the Law even offered a specific ritual by which the kinsman could get out of the obligation.

Naomi herself might have claimed the benefit of a levirate marriage if she were younger, and it would have been hard for Boaz to refuse since Naomi was a good and respected woman of Judah. The whole point of a levirate marriage, however, was to raise up sons to be credited to a dead husband, and Naomi was past the age of childbearing. Therefore she could not ask for any kind of marriage.

Ruth also had a claim. Boaz was a relative of her husband, Mahlon, the son of Naomi. What's more, she was young and pretty and could perfectly well bear a child.

But she was a Moabite girl. Boaz might be kind to her for Naomi's sake, but if she demanded a legal marriage, Boaz might suddenly remember she was a Moabite woman and be sufficiently angered by her presumption to drive her away.

Naomi had to be very careful, then, concerning the manner in which the whole thing was to be arranged. Ruth must wash and anoint herself with something nice-smelling, so as to make herself as pretty and as pleasant as possible. She must go to the threshing-floor, where she would be sure to find Boaz in a very good mood after the successful harvest, especially after he had had a good meal and a little wine.

Ruth must stay away from him while others were around in daylight. For her to push forward at that time would seem immodest. Furthermore, it would put Boaz in a bad position. He would feel he was being asked to make a difficult decision in public and he would resent that. And if he then turned her away publicly, Ruth would be forever shamed.

Ruth had to go to him privately, and at night. Then he could either accept his responsibility or reject it, and in either case, it could be done without public knowledge. But going to a man at night had certain risks also, and Naomi knew that.

As for Ruth, she was ready now, as always, to undergo any risk or difficulty for the good of her mother-in-law and for the name of her dead husband. If the appeal worked, not only she but Naomi, too, would have security, and the memory of Elimelech and of Mahlon would be perpetuated.

> **"I will do whatever you tell me," Ruth answered.
> So she went down to the threshing-floor and did exactly as her mother-in-law had told her.**
>
> **(Ruth 3:5–6)**

It must have been a difficult time for her. She had to go down while it was still daylight in order to be able to see where it would be that Boaz would lie down to sleep. (Those were simple times and threshing and winnowing took several days. The farmers slept in the fields as one way of guarding their grain.)

Ruth, dressed neatly and perfumed as well, had to try to keep her eye on Boaz and, at the same time, avoid receiving too much notice. Somehow, she managed. Probably she wore a hood, veiled herself closely, and talked to no one.

But then came the time:

> When Boaz had eaten and drunk, he felt at peace with the world and went to lie down at the far end of the heap of grain. She came in quietly, turned back the covering at his feet and lay down.
>
> (Ruth 3:7)

Quietly, Ruth lay there; tense, perhaps a little frightened. She did not quite dare to wake him. He might be startled enough to shout and rouse others and that would be unbearably embarrassing. If he were roused, he might be angry and refuse to listen to her. He might even draw a wrong conclusion and think that she had come to seduce him.

She decided to wait. Perhaps he would wake naturally during the night. That, indeed, was what happened.

> About midnight something disturbed the man as he slept; he turned over and, lo and behold, there was a woman lying at his feet. "Who are you?" he asked.
>
> (Ruth 3:8–9a)

Ruth had to speak now, quietly, quickly, and to the point. She had to make Boaz aware of exactly what was at stake and what she had in mind, before he roused the others.

"I am your servant, Ruth," she replied. "Now
spread your skirt over your servant, because you are
my next-of-kin."

(Ruth 3:9b)

When she had first met Boaz in the field and had not
known he was a relative, she had asked not to be treated
as a servant. Now that she knew the relationship and
was asking a legal marriage, that he "spread his skirt
over" her (meaning, protect her and give her security)
she did not hesitate to present herself humbly as his
servant.

Boaz was a man of intelligence and he understood at
once. In fact, being a pious and kindly man, it may even
have occurred to him during the time of the harvest that
he might be asked to submit to a levirate marriage. It
might even be that, seeing and admiring Ruth, he did
not find the possibility distasteful.

And yet he may well have hung back. He was a
prosperous man, but he was no longer young, and probably he was not particularly handsome. The Bible does
not say whether he was married, but few men in those
days remained unmarried. However, life was often short
and it might be that his wife and sons, if any, were dead.
There is no way of telling.

Aware of his own shortcomings, he might have felt
hesitant about approaching Ruth. He was old and plain,
with none of the charm of youth. He might even remember
that the first time he spoke to Ruth, she was afraid he
might try to take her as a handmaiden so that she acted
as though he repelled her.

Why should she not try to entice some handsome young

man into marrying her for the pleasure that would give her? Of course, any children she had from such a marriage would not be entitled to the inheritance of Elimelech and Mahlon. Their names would not be perpetuated. What's more, Naomi would not be taken care of, for a young husband who was no relation would feel no responsibility for Naomi.

For Ruth to avoid young men and to approach old Boaz meant that she placed her family concerns and her love of her mother-in-law above personal desires perhaps.

> He said, "The Lord has blessed you, my daughter. This last proof of your loyalty is greater than the first; you have not sought after any young man, rich or poor. Set your mind at rest, my daughter. I will do whatever you ask; for, as the whole neighbourhood knows, you are a capable woman."
>
> (Ruth 3:10–11)

But Boaz was meticulous in his piety. He was willing to do his duty, but he could not do it with strict attention to the Law unless he were truly, as Naomi and Ruth thought, the next-of-kin. He, apparently, knew of a complication of which the women were not aware. He said:

> "Are you sure that I am the next-of-kin? There is a kinsman even closer than I. Spend the night here and then in the morning, if he is willing to act as your next-of-kin, well and good; but if he is not willing, I will do so; I swear it by the Lord. Now lie down till morning."
>
> (Ruth 3:12–13)

Boaz was as concerned for Ruth's reputation as she herself was. He did not want anyone to know she had been there in the night lest wrong conclusions be drawn:

> So she lay at his feet till morning, but rose before one man could recognize another; and he said, "It must not be known that a woman has been to the threshing-floor."
>
> (Ruth 3:14)

She was to leave in the dark, just as she had come in the dark. Nor would he let her go home empty-handed.

> Then he said, "Bring me the cloak you have on, and hold it out." So she held it out, and he put in six measures of barley and lifted it on her back, and she went to town.
>
> (Ruth 3:15)

Once again Naomi was waiting anxiously. We can be pretty sure she had spent a sleepless night.

> When she came to her mother-in-law, Naomi asked, "How did things go with you, my daughter?" Ruth told her all that the man had done for her. "He gave me these six measures of barley," she said; "he would not let me come home to my mother-in-law empty-handed."
>
> (Ruth 3:16–17)

Naomi was satisfied; in fact, more than satisfied. Boaz would not have been so kind if he had not felt the matter of the levirate marriage to fit in with his own desires. He was a man of business, used to making decisions. He would not let matters hang.

> Naomi answered, "Wait, my daughter, until you see what will come of it. He will not rest until he has settled the matter today."
>
> (Ruth 3:18)

# CHAPTER 8

# BOAZ TAKES OVER

Naomi was quite right. Boaz did not even wait to finish threshing. He must have left that in the hands of his overseer for he seems to have gone to Bethlehem at once.

> **Now Boaz had gone up to the city gate, and was sitting there . . .**
>
> **(Ruth 4:1a)**

The gate of the town was the logical place to sit. Every town in those days had to be protected from raiders and from enemy armies. The towns therefore had walls around them, walls which were difficult for the enemy to climb over or break through against strongly fighting defenders.

The walls of a town have to have gates, just as the walls of a house have to have doors. A small town like Bethlehem might have only one gate. A larger one might have two. Jerusalem had seven gates in its days as capital of Judah.

These gates had large bronze doors that could be closed at sunset and opened at daybreak. Or at least they were opened at daybreak if there was peace in the land.

The gates were always busy places, of course, because everyone who wanted to enter the city or leave it had to pass through the gate. Merchants from far places would come with their caravans and would have to be inspected by the guards to make sure they had come in peace. Travelers who wanted to stop for the night before continuing onward would come to the gate.

People from the city would sit at the gate too, if they had some spare time. There they could meet travelers and hear the news from other towns and places (for, of course, there were no newspapers in those days). They could meet the merchants when they arrived and could look over the goods they had for sale. They could meet with other people from the city who had also come to be at the gate.

Inside the gate there was usually a large clear area on which no houses were allowed to be built. That was necessary in wartime because the armed defenders of the city would have to be gathered there to prevent the enemy from breaking in; or to make ready a charge outside that would strike the enemy unexpectedly.

In peacetime this cleared area was useful too. Merchants arriving with their laden camels, or other beasts of burden, could set up stalls in the area inside the wall and make it into a market place. The people of the city could gather in times of peace to consider some emergency measure, some new law, some trial of lawbreakers.

The city gate was a market place, an assembly place, a law court, a gathering place of all kinds.

If any man in Bethlehem wanted to meet another man and didn't know where he was, he had only to post himself at the city gate and sooner or later, probably sooner, the other would pass. And that was what Boaz did. Early in the day he placed himself at the city gate and kept a keen eye out for that person who was a closer kinsman to the family of Elimelech than he himself was. It didn't take long:

> **. . . and, after a time, the next-of-kin of whom he had spoken passed by. "Here," he cried, calling him by name, "come and sit down." He came and sat down.**
>
> **(Ruth 4:1b)**

What Boaz intended was to come to some formal agreement, one which the other could not change later on. Therefore he needed witnesses, and the most important ones he could find too. The city gate was the best place for that, for one could almost always find the old men of the town there.

These men were too old for hard labor in the fields, so they would certainly not be out on the threshing-floor; nor would they be in the shops or business places of the city. Indeed, old men were valued in those days for the fact that they could remember how things were many years before. They usually had the best knowledge of the customs and laws of the neighborhood, of past judgments and decisions.

There were no written laws in those days, no law books. People had to rely on the memory of old men with judgment and experience. They were the elders of the town who were looked up to and respected. Of course, they would be at the city gate, where their knowledge might be needed and wanted at any time.

> Then Boaz stopped ten elders of the town, and asked them to sit there, and they did so.
>
> (Ruth 4:2)

By that time, everyone in the market place near the city gate could see that Boaz must have had something important on his mind and they must have gathered round curiously. This suited Boaz. The more people were present to witness, the better.

Boaz began to explain matters to his relative in the presence and hearing of all:

> Then he said to the next-of-kin, "You will remember the strip of field that belonged to our brother Elimelech. Naomi has returned from the Moabite country and is selling it. I promised to open the matter with you, to ask you to acquire it in the presence of those who sit here, in the presence of the elders of my people. If you are going to do your duty as next-of-kin, then do so, but if not, someone must do it. So tell me, and then I shall know; for I come after you as next-of-kin."
>
> (Ruth 4:3–4a)

This seemed clear enough. There was land that belonged to Elimelech to begin with and then to his sons and all were dead. Naomi could not properly inherit it and if nobody came to her help, almost anyone might simply seize it. Not only would it be lost to Naomi, but to the family as well.

However, if someone from the family bought it, it would be saved for the family. What's more the family representative ought to be willing to pay a good price for it, to help Naomi. A stranger might not be willing to do so, but a next-of-kin would.

The next-of-kin probably did not think that this was a particularly good business venture. He might simply have claimed the land as his without payment since he was the nearest male member of the family after Elimelech and his sons. Or else, if he had not wished to be so cruel as to leave Naomi penniless, he might have bargained with her in private. Surely, poverty would have forced her to part with the land for a sum that would have represented a bargain for the buyer.

But now here was Boaz frowning at him and ten elders watching, and many men from the city listening. What could he do?

**He answered, "I will act as next-of-kin."**

**(Ruth 4:4b)**

Boaz listened to that and waited a moment. He must have known that it was a hard thing for the next-of-kin to agree to carry out a financial transaction which would probably represent a loss to him. Now was the time to hit him with something even worse.

> Then Boaz said, "On the day when you acquire the
> field from Naomi, you also acquire Ruth the Moab-
> itess, the dead man's wife, so as to perpetuate the
> name of the dead man with his patrimony."
>
> (Ruth 4:5)

That was something new and unexpected. The next-of-kin had heard the mention of Naomi and had known that he couldn't be expected to marry her, for she was too old to bear children. He would simply pay her money and that would be it.

He had forgotten about Ruth. Or else, because she was a Moabite woman, he had assumed she didn't count.

But, of course, Ruth had been the wife of Mahlon, the older son of Elimelech, and it was only through her that children could be raised to the family of Elimelech.

To the next-of-kin, this was an awful situation. It was bad enough paying a premium price for a piece of land, but now he would have to take a wife too. Undoubtedly he had one already, perhaps more than one, and a new young woman (and a pretty one too) would not be greeted gladly by his wife or wives. The fact that she was a Moabite woman would make things worse. In fact, Boaz had deliberately stressed that. He said that the minute the next-of-kin bought the field he also became responsible for "Ruth the Moabitess." He didn't let the other forget the nationality.

What's more, after the next-of-kin paid all that money for the property, it would not stay in his family. It would be inherited by the son or sons of Ruth, who would be counted to Elimelech's family.

He must have been able to hear the grumblings of his own sons in his imagination. He could hear them muttering that first he had bought the land with money that was really theirs, and then that land was to go to someone else.

The next-of-kin could not face that—

**Thereupon the next-of-kin said, "I cannot act myself, for I should risk losing my own patrimony. You must therefore do my duty as next-of-kin. I cannot act."**

**(Ruth 4:6)**

Boaz smiled. That was exactly what he had hoped would happen.

It was not absolutely necessary for the next-of-kin to do his duty. The Law explained how he could avoid it with reference to the brother of the widow's dead husband:

*But if the man is unwilling to take his brother's wife, she shall go to the elders at the town gate and say, "My husband's brother refuses to perpetuate his brother's name in Israel; he will not do his duty by me." At this the elders of the town shall summon him and reason with him. If he still stands his ground and says, "I will not take her," his brother's widow shall go up to him in the presence of the elders; she shall pull his sandal off his foot and spit in his face and declare: "Thus we requite the man who will not build up his brother's family." His family shall be known in Israel as the House of the Unsandalled Man.*
(Deuteronomy 25:7–10)

This was all designed to disgrace the man. By taking off his sandal, the woman might be indicating scornfully that the man was too poor to wear sandals. (Only the poorest people went barefoot.) After all, he did not feel rich enough to care for his brother's widow. Another possibility is that by taking off his sandal, the widow denied him the right to walk on the property of the dead man.

Probably many a person who did not really wish to do his duty by his brother's widow did it anyway rather than submit to such disgrace in the eyes of all the town.

Of course, Boaz wasn't interested in disgracing the next-of-kin. He wanted to make it as easy as possible for him to allow Boaz to take over. If he were disgraced, spat at, called names, he might change his mind and say that he would marry Ruth, and certainly Boaz didn't want that. So Boaz meant to go through only the barest minimum of the ritual.

Yet the Writer felt called upon to explain that ritual. After all, polygamy was no longer allowed, and levirate marriage was no longer the custom. Ordinary people in the time of the Writer, who had not studied the Law carefully, wouldn't even remember the matter of the sandal being taken off, so the Writer had to explain it. But he explained only the gentle way in which Boaz planned to carry it through:

> Now in those old days, when property was re-deemed or exchanged, it was the custom for a man to pull off his sandal and give it to the other party. This was the form of attestation in Israel. So the next-of-

kin said to Boaz, "Acquire it for yourself," and pulled
off his sandal.

(Ruth 4:7–8)

The next-of-kin pulled it off himself gently. It was not
taken from him with force and scorn by the woman he
had refused. There was no spitting. Boaz did no more,
probably, than take the sandal politely and hold it high
for everyone to see.

> Then Boaz declared to the elders and all the peo-
> ple, "You are witnesses today that I have acquired
> from Naomi all that belonged to Elimelech and all
> that belonged to Mahlon and Chilion; and, further,
> that I have myself acquired Ruth the Moabitess, wife
> of Mahlon, to be my wife, to perpetuate the name of
> the deceased with his patrimony, so that his name
> may not be missing among his kindred and at the
> gate of his native place. You are witnesses this day."
> (Ruth 4:9–10)

Boaz had accomplished what he had set out to do. He
knew he would now have the loyal, modest, and virtuous
Ruth as his wife. She knew that she would be the wife of
the most respected man in Bethlehem, and the kindest too.
And she knew that her beloved mother-in-law would be
taken care of. And as for Naomi, she had seen to it that
the daughter-in-law who had so loyally followed her out
of Moab was secure.

Moreover, everyone at the gate seemed pleased. They
approved the transaction with what was the kind of blessing appropriate for a marriage that was to take place:

> Then the elders and all who were at the gate said,
> "We are witnesses. May the Lord make this woman,
> who has come to your home, like Rachel and Leah,
> the two who built up the house of Israel. May you do
> great things in Ephrathah and keep a name alive in
> Bethlehem. May your house be like the house of
> Perez, whom Tamar bore to Judah, through the off-
> spring the Lord will give you by this girl."
>
> (Ruth 4:11–12)

Rachel and Leah were the two wives of Jacob (also
known as Israel). Each of them had a servant whom
they offered to Jacob as an additional wife. Rachel and
Leah and the two servants bore a total of twelve sons to
Jacob, and these were the ancestors of the twelve tribes
of Israel.

Perez was the son of Judah who had been born of a
levirate marriage and Boaz himself was a descendant of
him. The elders were hoping that he would continue the
house worthily and his manner of doing so was next to
be described.

> So Boaz took Ruth and made her his wife. When
> they came together, the Lord caused her to conceive
> and she bore Boaz a son.
>
> (Ruth 4:13)

That, in a way, is a happy ending for Ruth, for every
woman in Israel and Judah wanted a son.

And since this son was counted to Elimelech, it meant
that he was, legally, Naomi's grandson, and at last she

had a male offspring to replace the two who had died. All her friends joined her in her happiness.

> **Then the women said to Naomi, "Blessed be the Lord today, for he has not left you without a next-of-kin. May the dead man's name be kept alive in Israel."**
>
> **(Ruth 4:14)**

They were hoping that the son would have a son, who would also have a son, and so on, so that the name of Elimelech would be kept alive in memory. They were also aware that this meant that Naomi's position was secure, because a grandson, grown-up and strong, would be bound to support Naomi in her extreme old age, for she would be his grandmother. The women said:

> **"The child will give you new life and cherish you in your old age; for your daughter-in-law who loves you, who has proved better to you than seven sons, has borne him."**
>
> **(Ruth 4:15)**

This is really Ruth's reward. She had come to Bethlehem a foreigner; worse than an ordinary foreigner, for she was a Moabite woman. Yet she was now accepted, not only by Boaz but by all the women of the city, for her loyalty and love.

In fact, in a society which thought so highly of sons and so little of daughters, the women still had to admit that Ruth was better to Naomi than seven sons would have been. What a testimonial to the wonderful goodness of this girl.

We can be sure Naomi could barely allow anyone else to touch the young child, not even its own mother:

> **Naomi took the child and laid him in her lap and become his nurse. Her neighbours gave him a name: "Naomi has a son," they said, "we will call him Obed."**
>
> **(Ruth 4:16–17a)**

They were acknowledging the relationship of Obed to the family of Elimelech.

And the story has a happy ending not only for the individuals in it, but for all of Judah, for the Writer goes on to explain in a few words concerning this child Obed:

> **He was the father of Jesse, the father of David.**
>
> **(Ruth 4:17b)**

CHAPTER 9

# A FINAL WORD

The book ends with a summary of the ancestry of the great king, David. Perhaps the Writer put it in himself, or perhaps a later editor put it in. It goes:

> **This is the genealogy of Perez: Perez was the father of Hezron, Hezron of Ram, Ram of Amminadab, Amminadab of Nahshon, Nahshon of Salmon, Salmon of Boaz, Boaz of Obed, Obed of Jesse, and Jesse of David.**
>
> **(Ruth 4:18–22)**

Now after reading the tale of Ruth, anyone looking at the genealogy would know something at once. He would know that it continued all the way to David only because Boaz had been kind enough and decent enough to accept a Moabite girl as his wife for her virtue and loyalty.

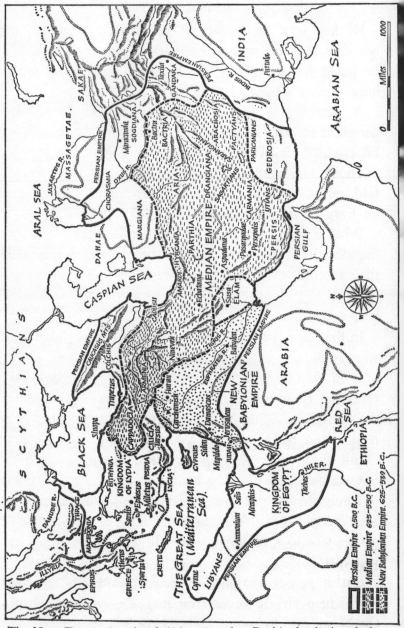

The Near East as it existed 600 years after Ruth's death, just before the book of Ruth was written.

He had seen the beauty of her character and he did not care that she was a foreigner who was supposed to be hated for something her ancestors were supposed to have done a century before.

A person was to be considered for himself or for herself, and not for anything else, not for his neighbors, his country, or his ancestors.

Those who read the story of Ruth, or listened to it told, might well have wondered: What if there had been an Ezra in Boaz's time?

What if Ezra had come into the market place and had thundered that all the men of the city must put away their foreign wives; that Boaz must not dare marry Ruth; or that he must divorce her if he had already married her, and disown Obed if Obed had already been born?

In that case there would never have been a David. And what would the history of Judah have been without David?

If in the time of Ezra and of the Writer, the Jews returning to Jerusalem never dared welcome strangers to their midst; never dared intermarry with them; what great men would never come to be born?

But the Writer did not persuade everybody. He did not win out; Ezra did. The Jews continued to be suspicious of foreigners. So did most other people of the time. So do most people today. We ourselves are often suspicious of people who look different, who talk differently, who aren't just like ourselves.

But it is not too late to learn the lesson of Ruth. Somewhere among those strangers may be many Ruths. Ought we not to try to find them? Should we not look at each person closely, as an individual with his own virtues and faults, and judge him for that and not for anything else.

And if we could find all the Ruths of the world, how much better off all of us would be.

Widely known for both his science fiction and his serious scientific essays, ISAAC ASIMOV has written over one hundred and twenty books on subjects ranging from physics to mythology, from mathematics to the Bible. Born in Russia in 1920, Dr. Asimov came to Brooklyn with his family at the age of three, received his Ph.D. from Columbia University in 1948, and in the following year joined the faculty of Boston University School of Medicine. He now lives in New York City.